INSTRUCTIONS: Insert this Supplement in the pocket provided in the back of the main volume. All material in this Supplement is keyed to pages and Sections of the main volume.

UNDERSTANDING CRIMINAL PROCEDURE

1992–1993 SUPPLEMENT

D0125284

. . .ojessor of Law
Wayne State University

> **LEGAL TEXT SERIES**

1992

 **Matthew Bender**

Times Mirror Books

UNDERSTANDING CRIMINAL PROCEDURE

1992–1993 SUPPLEMENT

Joshua Dressler
Professor of Law
Wayne State University

LEGAL TEXT SERIES

1992

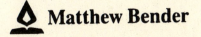

Matthew Bender

Times Mirror
Books

MATTHEW BENDER & CO., INC.
EDITORIAL OFFICES
11 PENN PLAZA, NEW YORK, NY 10001–2006 (212) 967-7707
2101 WEBSTER STREET, OAKLAND, CA 94612–3027 (510) 446-7100

LEGAL EDUCATION PUBLICATIONS

ADVISORY BOARD

PREFACE

This pocket part covers all of the important United States Supreme Court cases decided after the Main Volume went to print, through the end of the 1991–1992 term. Also included are citations to significant lower federal and state court opinions, and to new scholarly literature published in the field.

I have tried to give readers what they need to be up–to–date, while remaining sensitive to the importance of keeping down the size, and thus the cost, of the Supplement.

I welcome suggestions on ways to improve the product. I also invite your comments on the Main Volume.

Joshua Dressler
Wayne State University
Detroit, Michigan 48202

September 1, 1992

TABLE OF CONTENTS

Page

Chapter 9
FOURTH AMENDMENT: "PROBABLE CAUSE"

Chapter 10
SEARCH WARRANTS: IN GENERAL

Chapter 11
ARRESTS

Chapter 13
SEARCHES INCIDENT TO LAWFUL ARRESTS

Chapter 14
SEARCHES OF CARS AND CONTAINERS THEREIN

Chapter 15
THE "PLAIN VIEW" DOCTRINE

Chapter 16
INVENTORY SEARCHES

Chapter 17
CONSENT TO SEARCH

Chapter 18
MINIMALLY INTRUSIVE SEARCHES AND SEIZURES: THE *TERRY* PRINCIPLE

Chapter 19
"SPECIAL GOVERNMENTAL NEED" (FORMERLY, "ADMINISTRATIVE") SEARCHES

Chapter 20
FOURTH AMENDMENT: "STANDING"

Chapter 21
FOURTH AMENDMENT: EXCLUSIONARY RULE

Chapter 22
INTERROGATION LAW: OVERVIEW

Chapter 23
COERCED ("INVOLUNTARY") CONFESSIONS

Page

Chapter 29
THE RIGHT TO COUNSEL: AT TRIAL AND ON APPEAL

Chapter 30
PRETRIAL RELEASE OF THE DEFENDANT

Chapter 31
PLEA BARGAINING AND GUILTY PLEAS

Chapter 32
DOUBLE JEOPARDY

CHAPTER 1

INTRODUCTION TO CRIMINAL PROCEDURE

§ 2 Sources of Procedural Law

Page 2, add to footnote 9, at the end of the first sentence:

⁹ . . . Latzer, *The Hidden Conservatism of the State Court "Revolution"*, 74 Judicature 190 (1991) (providing a list, by state, of the number of cases in which each state's highest court has rejected or adopted United States Supreme Court's criminal procedure decisions, from the late 1960s through 1989). . . .

§ 3 Stages of a Criminal Prosecution

Page 5, end of subsection [C][2], add new footnote 14.1:

In many jurisdictions, . . . discussed immediately below.[14.1]

[14.1] Although *Gerstein* requires a prompt probable–cause determination, the Supreme Court ruled, 5–4, in County of Riverside v. McLaughlin, 111 S.Ct. 1661 (1991) that the Constitution "permits a reasonable postponement of a probable cause determination while the police cope with the everyday problems of processing suspects through an overly burdened criminal justice system." Therefore, the Court held, if a jurisdiction wishes to combine the *Gerstein* hearing with other pretrial proceedings, such as the initial arraignment, it may do so as long as the hearing occurs, as a general matter, within 48 hours (including weekends) from the time of arrest. However, a delay "for delay's sake," out of ill–will toward the suspect, or in order to secure evidence that will justify the arrest, is constitutionally unreasonable, even if it falls within the presumptive 48–hour period. The dissenters would have required the probable–cause hearing to be held within 24 hours of arrest.

Page 5, end of the first paragraph of subsection [C][3], add new footnote 15.1:

An arrested person . . . or "initial" "appearance."[15.1]

[15.1] In view of County of Riverside v. McLaughlin, 111 S.Ct. 1661 (1991), *see* n. 14.1 *supra*, it remains to be seen whether courts, commanded by statute or procedural rule to bring the arrested party before the magistrate for her first appearance "without unnecessary delay," will now permit two–day, rather than one–day, delays. As Justice Scalia pointed out in dissent in *McLaughlin*, however, "'[w]ith one exception, no federal court considering the question has regarded 24 hours as an inadequate amount of time to complete arrest procedures. . . .'"

Page 9, end of the second paragraph, add new footnote 40.1:

Although the prosecutor . . . of her race.[40.1]

[40.1] Since publication of the Main Volume, the Supreme Court has greatly expanded the scope of the *Batson* rule. First, in Powers v. Ohio, 111 S.Ct. 1364 (1991), it ruled that the equal protection clause bars a prosecutor from using racially discriminatory peremptory challenges, even if the defendant and excluded jurors are *not* of the same race. Thus, in *Powers*, a *white* defendant in a murder trial was permitted to challenge the prosecutor's peremptory challenges of prospective *black* jurors. According to *Powers*, *Batson* "was designed 'to serve multiple ends,' only one of which was to protect individual defendants from discrimination in the selection of jurors." *Batson* "recognized that a prosecutor's discriminatory use of peremptory challenges harms the excluded jurors and the community at large." *Powers* reasoned that a defendant is injured by race–based exclusions of prospective jurors, even if she is not of the same race as the excluded jurors, because the discrimination "places the fairness of a criminal proceeding in doubt." Also, by permitting the defendant to object to the prosecutor's actions, the right of the excluded person to serve on juries is more satisfactorily enforced.

Second, in Edmonson v. Leesville Concrete Co., 111 S.Ct. 2077 (1991), the justices applied *Batson* in a civil trial context, ruling that the defendant–corporation in a personal injury law suit brought by a black plaintiff could not use peremptory challenges to exclude jurors on account of their race. Borrowing from *Powers*, the Court reasoned that such exclusions violated the equal protection rights of the challenged jurors.

Third, the Supreme Court extended *Batson* to defense attorneys in criminal trials in Georgia v. McCollum, 112 S.Ct. 2348 (1992). In *McCollum*, white defendants were charged with assaulting two African–Americans. The prosecutor requested the trial court to prohibit the defendants from exercising their peremptories to exclude black persons from the jury solely on the basis of race. When the trial court denied the motion, the state appealed. The Supreme Court held that exercise of racially discriminatory peremptory challenges by a defense attorney inflicts the same harms as those addressed in *Batson* and *Powers*. And, although the Constitution only prohibits racial discrimination attributable to state action, the Court concluded that, as in *Edmonson*, state action is present when a private defense attorney exercises peremptories, in part because it is the state that allows such challenges, and also because the courtroom setting in which the challenges are exercised creates the perception of governmental approval of the discriminatory conduct.

Page 10, add to footnote 48:

[48] . . . Patchel, *The New Habeas*, 42 Hastings L.J. 939 (1991); Rosenberg, *Kaddish for Federal Habeas Corpus*, 59 Geo. Wash. L. Rev. 362 (1991).

§ 4 Studying Constitutional Law Cases

Page 15, line 2, immediately preceding footnote 58, add the following new text:

In June, 1991, Justice Thurgood Marshall, one of the two remaining members of the Warren Court, retired. President Bush nominated, and the Senate approved, Judge Clarence Thomas, of the United States Court of Appeals, to replace Justice Marshall.

Page 15, add at the end of footnote 58:

[58] . . . For a recent study of the racial, religious, gender, and professional characteristics of the persons appointed to the federal bench by the Bush Administration, and a comparison of "Bush appointees" to those of the preceding five Presidents, *see* Goldman, *The Bush Imprint on the Judiciary: Carrying on a Tradition*, 74 Judicature 294 (1991).

CHAPTER 2

OVERARCHING POLICY ISSUES IN CRIMINAL PROCEDURE

§ 5 "Due Process" versus "Crime Control"

Page 17, add to footnote 1:

[1] . . . Dripps, *Beyond the Warren Court and Its Conservative Critics: Toward a Unified Theory of Constitutional Criminal Procedure*, 23 U. Mich. J.L. Ref. 591 (1990).

§ 6 The Value of "Truth" In the Criminal Justice System

Page 20, add to footnote 10:

[10] . . . Dripps, n. 1 (Pock. Pt.) *supra*; Rosenberg & Rosenberg, *Guilt: Henry Friendly Meets the MaHaRal of Prague*, 90 Mich. L. Rev. 604 (1991); Stacy, *The Search for the Truth in Constitutional Criminal Procedure*, 91 Colum. L. Rev. 1369 (1991).

§ 7 Accusatorial versus Inquisitorial Systems of Justice

Page 22, line 4 from the bottom of the page, add new footnote 28.1:

Sloganeering aside, . . . not purely accusatorial.[28.1]

[28.1] *See* McNeil v. Wisconsin, 111 S.Ct. 2204, 2210 n.2 (1991) ("Our system of justice is, and has always been, an inquisitorial one at the investigatory stage. . . .").

(Matthew Bender & Co., Inc.)   (Pub. 791)

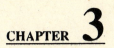

CHAPTER **3**

INCORPORATION OF THE BILL OF RIGHTS

§ 8 The Issue of Incorporation

Page 25, add to footnote 1:

[1] . . . Amar, *The Bill of Rights and the Fourteenth Amendment*, 101 Yale L.J. 1193 (1992).

CHAPTER 4

GENERAL CONSTITUTIONAL LAW DOCTRINES

§ 11 Retroactivity

Page 33, add to footnote 1:

[1] . . . Fallon, Jr. & Meltzer, *New Law, Non–Retroactivity, and Constitutional Remedies*, 104 Harv. L. Rev. 1731 (1991).

Page 37, add the following new text and footnotes at the end of subsection [b]:

The line between a "new rule" — one that is not "dictated" by an earlier holding — and a rule that "reasonable jurists" would agree is "compelled by earlier precedent" is difficult to draw.

For example, in *Butler v. McKellar*,[30.1] the Supreme Court concluded that a prior decision (call it *Case 2*) announced a "new rule" (and, therefore, could not be applied retroactively since it was decided after the petitioner's conviction became final), although it admittedly was "controlled" by an earlier decision (*Case 1*), which was decided before the petitioner's conviction became final. The *Butler* Court held that the rule announced in *Case 2* was not "dictated" by *Case 1*, as evidenced in part by the fact that prior to *Case 2* a "significant difference of opinion [existed] on the part of several lower courts" regarding the import of *Case 1* as to the issues decided in *Case 2*.

Does this analysis imply that a rule is "new" simply because a stray lower court opinion or two can be found that, subsequent to *Case 1* but prior to *Case 2*, reached a result contrary to the Supreme Court's later holding in *Case 2*? No, according to *Stringer v. Black*:[30.2]

> The purpose of the new rule doctrine is to validate reasonable interpretations of existing precedents. Reasonableness . . . is an objective standard, and the ultimate decision whether [*Case 2*] was dictated by precedent [*Case 1*] is based on an objective reading of the relevant cases. The short answer to the State's argument [that *Case 2* announced a new rule, as evidenced by the fact that one lower federal court read *Case 1* differently than did the Supreme Court subsequently in *Case 2*] is that the [lower court] made a serious mistake.

[30.1] 494 U.S. 407, *reh'g denied*, 495 U.S. 915 (1990).
[30.2] 112 S.Ct. 1130, 1140 (1992).

(Matthew Bender & Co., Inc.)   (Pub. 791)

§ 13 Harmless Error

Page 40, add to footnote 51:

[51] . . . Arizona v. Fulminante, 111 S.Ct. 1246, *reh'g denied*, 111 S.Ct. 2067 (1991) (introduction at trial of a coerced confession); Yates v. Evatt, 111 S.Ct. 1884 (1991) (jury instruction improperly shifting the burden of proof of an element of the crime to the defendant, in violation of the due process clause).

Page 41, at the end of the first paragraph of subsection [C], add the following new text and footnote:

. . . In the past, the Court eschewed any neat classification system for determining which errors constitute *per se* prejudicial constitutional error. In general, errors were held to be prejudicial *per se* in the two types of circumstances described in the text of the Main Volume, immediately following this "pocket part" addition.

However, in *Arizona v. Fulminante*,[54.1] five justices (Chief Justice Rehnquist, and Justices O'Connor, Scalia, Kennedy and Souter) announced a new system for categorizing constitutional errors for purposes of harmless–error analysis. Under the new classification system, a "trial error," *i.e.*, an "error which occurred during the presentation of the case to the jury, and which may therefore be quantitatively assessed in the context of other evidence presented in order to determine whether its admission was harmless beyond a reasonable doubt," is tested under the *Chapman* harmless-error rule.

Only "structural defects in the constitution of the trial mechanism" constitute *per se* prejudicial error. The *per se* rule applies in such circumstances because a structural defect in the trial mechanism renders the proceeding inevitably unreliable. Although the classification system announced in this case is new, all of the examples of *per se* error mentioned in the Main Volume fall within the new "structural defect" (*per se* error) category, with the exception of the coerced–confession rule mentioned at footnote 57.

[54.1] Arizona v. Fulminante, 111 S.Ct. 1246, *reh'g denied*, 111 S.Ct. 2067 (1991).

Page 41, add at the end of footnote 57:

[57] . . . The Court answered the question affirmatively in *Fulminante*, 111 S.Ct. 1246, *reh'g denied*, 111 S.Ct. 2067 (1991). Applying the new classification system discussed in the text accompanying footnote 54.1, a majority concluded that the admission of a coerced confession is "classic 'trial error'," to which the *Chapman* harmless–error rule applies.

§ 14 Supervisory Power

Page 43, line 3, add new footnote 71.1:

Supervisory rulings intended . . . according to Beale.[71.1]

[71.1] *But see* United States v. Williams, 112 S.Ct. 1735 (1992), in which the Court, apparently with approval, described its supervisory power in broader terms:

That power has been applied not only to improve the truth–finding process of the trial, . . . but also to prevent parties from reaping benefit or incurring harm from violations of substantive or procedural rules (imposed by the Constitution or laws) governing matters apart from the trial itself. . . .

CHAPTER 7

FOURTH AMENDMENT
TERMINOLOGY: "SEARCH"

§ 32   Surveillance of Conversations By "False Friends"

Page 67, at the end of section 32, add new footnote 52.1:

The fear of . . . liberates daily life."[52.1]

[52.1] *See* State v. Blow, 602 A.2d 552 (Vt. 1991) (rejecting in part the rule in *White*, holding that electronic participant monitoring conducted in a person's home offends the core values of the state constitution and, therefore, ordinarily requires a search warrant).

§ 34   Technological Information–Gathering

Page 70, add at the end of footnote 65:

[65] . . . *Contra* under the state constitution, People v. Jackson, 116 Ill.App.3d 430, 72 Ill.Dec. 153, 452 N.E.2d 85 (1983); Commonwealth v. DeJohn, 486 Pa. 32, 403 A.2d 1283 (1979), *cert. denied*, 444 U.S. 1032 (1980); State v. Thompson, 810 P.2d 415 (Utah 1991) (all holding that customers have a reasonable expectation of privacy in their bank records).

§ 36   Testing for Contraband

Page 74, add at the end of footnote 84:

[84] . . . *Contra* under the state constitution, Pooley v. State, 705 P.2d 1293 (Alaska App. 1985) (dog sniff of luggage is a "search," requiring reasonable suspicion to conduct); McGahan v. State, 807 P.2d 506 (Alaska App. 1991) (*id.*, dog sniff of the exterior of a commercial building); People v. Dunn, 77 N.Y.2d 19, 563 N.Y.S.2d 388, 564 N.E.2d 1054 (1990), *cert. denied*, 111 S.Ct. 2830 (1991) (dog sniff of contraband outside a residence constitutes a "search," requiring reasonable suspicion to conduct).

Page 75, end of subsection [A], add new footnote 84.1:

We are aware . . . by the procedure."[84.1]

[84.1] "Police dogs that sniff drugs may soon find themselves out of a job." *The New York Times*, Oct. 9, 1991, C7, col. 1. According to the newspaper, a portable drug-detection system has been developed that can identify vapors from minuscule particles of illegal drugs. With the new system, a 15,000 square–foot workplace can be inexpensively and quickly tested for drugs, as can be smaller areas, such as a doorknob or desk top.

(Matthew Bender & Co., Inc.)   (Pub. 791)

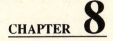

FOURTH AMENDMENT TERMINOLOGY: "SEIZURE"

§ 40 "Seizure" of Persons

Page 79, add to footnote 10:

[10] . . . Bacigal, *In Pursuit of the Elusive Fourth Amendment: The Police Chase Cases*, 58 Tenn. L. Rev. 73 (1990); Butterfoss, *Bright Line Seizures: The Need for Clarity in Determining When Fourth Amendment Activity Begins*, 79 J. Crim. L. & Criminology 437 (1988); Clancy, *The Future of Fourth Amendment Seizure Analysis After Hodari D. and Bostick*, 28 Am. Crim. L. Rev. 799 (1991); LaFave, *Pinguitudinous Police, Pachydermatous Prey: Whence Fourth Amendment "Seizures"?*, 1991 U. Ill. L. Rev. 729 (1991); Maclin, *"Black and Blue Encounters" — Some Preliminary Thoughts About Fourth Amendment Seizures: Should Race Matter?*, 26 Val. U. L. Rev. 243 (1991).

Page 79, add to footnote 12:

[12] . . . The "reasonable person" in this test "presupposes an innocent person." Florida v. Bostick, 111 S.Ct. 2382, 2388 (1991). The Supreme Court has never suggested that the "reasonable person" possesses the same racial characteristics as the person confronted by the police. However, one commentator believes that the objective test should be race–specific, because "the dynamics surrounding an encounter between a police officer and a black male are quite different from those that surround an encounter between an officer and the so–called average, reasonable person." Maclin, n. 10 (Pock. Pt.), *supra*, at 250. He contends that the ordinary encounter between a black male suspect and the police, even when the suspect is middle–class or professional, involves a degree of coercion ordinarily absent in other encounters.

Page 79, at the end of the first paragraph, add the following new text and footnote:

. . . In cases in which a person's freedom of movement is already restricted by a factor independent of police conduct, such as when he is seated in a cramped bus about to depart, "the appropriate inquiry is whether a reasonable person would feel free to decline the officers' requests or otherwise terminate the encounter."[12.1]

[12.1] Florida v. Bostick, 111 S.Ct. at 2387.

Page 80, at the end of the third paragraph of subsection [B], add the following new text and footnote:

. . . On the other hand, a request by an officer to search a person's luggage does not constitute a seizure, "as long as the police do not convey a message that compliance with their request is required."[28.1]

[28.1] Florida v. Bostick, 111 S.Ct. at 2386.

(Matthew Bender & Co., Inc.) (Pub. 791)

Page 81, end of subsection [B], add the following new text and footnotes:

Increasingly, "seizure" findings, such as in *Royer*, are the exception to the rule. For example, in *Florida v. Bostick*,[32.1] two sheriff's deputies boarded an interstate bus while it was temporarily stopped to pick up passengers, in order to intercept any drug traffickers who might be aboard. Dressed in "raid" jackets bearing the department's insignia, the deputies approached *D*, who was sitting in the back of the bus, identified themselves as narcotics agents, and questioned him. The deputies requested and received permission to search *D*'s luggage. The search turned up illegal drugs.

The state supreme court ruled that a reasonable person in *D*'s position would not have felt free to leave the bus, *i.e.*, *D* was "seized." Because the deputies concededly lacked any basis to suspect *D* before they seized him, the state court held that *D*'s subsequent consent to search his luggage was invalid.

The United States Supreme Court in *Bostick* did not determine whether *D* was seized; it remanded the case to the state court to evaluate the matter "under the correct legal standard." According to the Court, "the degree to which a reasonable person [in *D*'s position] would feel that he or she could leave is not an accurate measure of the coercive effect of the encounter." *D*'s feeling of confinement, the Court suggested, was "the natural result of his decision to take the bus." The proper test in such circumstances is whether "a reasonable person would feel free to decline the officers' requests or otherwise terminate the encounter."

Mendenhall, Delgado,[32.2] and *Bostick* in conjunction send a message to lower courts: absent the use of physical force by the police, the Supreme Court will rarely stand in their way if they treat virtually all police–citizen investigatory confrontations as "close encounters of the non-Fourth Amendment kind,"[32.3] *i.e.*, as non–"seizures" of the person.

[32.1] 111 S.Ct. 2382 (1991).

[32.2] *See* n. 32 *supra*.

[32.3] LaFave, n. 10 (Pock. Pt.) *supra*, at 737 (quoting Professor Yale Kamisar at the U.S. Law Week 13th Annual Constitutional Law Conference (Sept. 6, 1991)).

Pages 81–82, subsection [C], delete all of the text and accompanying footnotes after the first paragraph, and substitute the following new text and footnotes:

For example, suppose that the police see *D* standing on the sidewalk. When they turn in his direction, *D* flees. If the police pursue *D* by car or on foot, is he "seized" the moment the pursuit begins, or only if and when he is captured? Or, might a "seizure" occur at some intermediate stage, on a case–by–case basis?

The issue is significant because, if a pursuit is not a "seizure," the police may (from a Fourth Amendment perspective) chase someone without any basis for believing that he is involved in wrongdoing. Furthermore, if the pursued party discards an object during the chase, the police may retrieve it without the latter action constituting a fruit of an unlawful seizure.

In *Michigan v. Chesternut*,[33] the Court rejected competing bright-line arguments

[33] 486 U.S. 567 (1988).

fashioned for them, *i.e.*, that all pursuits are seizures (the defendant's position) and that a seizure only occurs upon capture (the government's position). Instead, the Court adhered to its "traditional contextual approach," whereby the question of whether and when a seizure has occurred is determined on a case–by–case basis.

In *Chesternut*, the Court concluded that the officers' pursuit of the individual (they drove alongside the suspect, who was moving on foot) was not so intimidating that it communicated to a reasonable person in *D's* situation "an attempt to capture or otherwise intrude upon [*D's*] freedom of movement." In dictum, however, the Court suggested that the result might have been different if the officers had used their siren, drawn their guns, or "operated the car in an aggressive manner to block [*D's*] course or otherwise control the direction or speed of his movements." In other words, upon the right facts, an "attempt to capture" could constitute a "seizure."

However, in *California v. Hodari D.*,[34] the Court held that a person is not "seized" unless the officer physically touches the pursued suspect or the subject submits to the officer's assertion of authority. Speaking for the majority, Justice Scalia stated:

> The word "seizure" readily bears the meaning of a laying on of hands or application of physical force to restrain movement, even when it is ultimately unsuccessful. ("She seized the purse–snatcher, but he broke out of her grasp.") It does not remotely apply, however, to the prospect of a policeman yelling "Stop, in the name of the law!" at a fleeing form that continues to flee. That is no seizure. . . . [A seizure] requires either physical force . . . or, where that is absent, *submission* to the assertion of authority.

According to the Court, "neither usage nor common–law tradition makes an attempted seizure a seizure."

The Court distinguished *Chesternut* on the ground that, on the facts of the pursuit in that case, a reasonable person would not have believed that the officers had conveyed the message that the suspect was not free to go about his business. As Justice Scalia explained, "[w]e did not address in *Chesternut* . . . the question whether, if the *Mendenhall* [reasonable person] test was met — if the message that the defendant was not free to leave had been conveyed — a Fourth Amendment seizure would have occurred." In other words, in order for a "seizure" to occur in the absence of physical force: (1) the police must convey the message that the suspect is not free to go about his business, which is determined by application of the reasonable–person test; and (2) the suspect must stop, *i.e.*, submit to authority.

Justices Stevens and Marshall dissented. They accused the majority of "adopt[ing] a definition of 'seizure' that is unfaithful to a long line of Fourth Amendment cases," including *Mendenhall* and *Chesternut*.

They also attacked the ruling as "profoundly unwise." The dissenters' worry relates to the potentially "significant time interval between the initiation of the officer's show of [authority] and the complete submission by the citizen [when the 'seizure' occurs]." Following the majority's approach, the police may now lawfully chase a person — even if the pursuit includes a command to "freeze," the use of

---

[34] 111 S.Ct. 1547 (1991).

sirens, or other coercive actions — without reasonable suspicion of wrongdoing, in the hope that during the pursuit the suspect's response, *e.g.*, a furtive motion, will justify the subsequent seizure.[35] Yet, anomalously, if an officer barely touches the suspect in an effort to detain him, but the citizen escapes, such "laying on of hands" is a "seizure," and, the subsequent furtive behavior by the citizen cannot be used to justify the prior seizure.[36]

---

[35] Does unprovoked flight justify a subsequent seizure? The Court hinted that it might. *See* § 95[B] (Pock. Pt.), *infra*.

[36] Professor LaFave, only somewhat tongue–in–cheek, suggests that the message of *Hodari D.* to police departments is that when the police chase a person on a hunch, a "fat cop" is preferable to one of "slim, trim, and of athletic build," because the latter officer is too likely to catch up to the suspect and grab him "by the scruff of the neck *before* the [contraband is] ditched." LaFave, n. 10 (Pock. Pt.) *supra*, at 730, 731.

CHAPTER 9

FOURTH AMENDMENT: "PROBABLE CAUSE"

§ 46 The *Gates* "Totality of the Circumstances" Test

Page 97, add at the end of footnote 72:

[72] . . . In 1991, however, the Connecticut Supreme Court reversed itself and ruled that local courts should hereafter apply the *Gates* test. State v. Barton, 219 Conn. 529, 594 A.2d 917 (1991), *overruling* State v. Kimbro, 197 Conn. 219, 496 A.2d 498 (1985).

§ 48 "Probable Cause": A Sliding Scale?

Page 101, add at the end of footnote 96:

[96] . . . *See* United States v. Chaidez, 919 F.2d 1193, 1197 (7th Cir. 1990), *cert. denied*, 112 S.Ct. 209 (1991) (favoring a sliding–scale approach, the court observed that "circumstances defy . . . simple categorization, and if a [probable–cause] line must nonetheless be drawn it will be arbitrary, with nearly identical cases on opposite sides"); *see also* Slobogin, *The World Without a Fourth Amendment*, 39 UCLA L. Rev. 1, 38–78 (1991) (advocating a sliding–scale — "proportionality principle" — approach to the Fourth Amendment).

CHAPTER 10

SEARCH WARRANTS: IN GENERAL

§ 49 The Constitutional Role of the Search Warrant

Page 103, add to footnote 1:

[1] . . . Bookspan, *Reworking the Warrant Requirement: Resuscitating the Fourth Amendment*, 44 Vand. L. Rev. 473 (1991); Green, *"Power, Not Reason": Justice Marshall's Valedictory and the Fourth Amendment in the Supreme Court's 1990 Term*, 70 N.C. L. Rev. 373 (1992); Stuntz, *Warrants and Fourth Amendment Remedies*, 77 Va. L. Rev. 881 (1991); Slobogin, *The World Without a Fourth Amendment*, 39 UCLA L. Rev. 1 (1991).

Page 103, end of subsection [A], add new footnote 3.1:

As is discussed . . . has been inconsistent.[3.1]

[3.1] *See* California v. Acevedo, 111 S.Ct. 1982, 1992 (1991) (Scalia, J., concurring in the judgment) ("[O]ur jurisprudence [has] lurched back and forth between imposing a categorical warrant requirement and looking to reasonableness alone.").

Page 104, add at the end of footnote 11:

[11] . . . . *See* California v. Acevedo, 111 S.Ct. 1982, 1994 (1991) (Stevens and Marshall, JJ., dissenting):

> [H]istory is, however, only part of the explanation for the warrant requirement. The requirement also reflects the sound policy judgment that, absent exceptional circumstances, the decision to invade the privacy of an individual's personal effects should be made by a neutral magistrate rather than an agent of the Executive.

Page 105, add at the end of footnote 22:

[22] . . . Since Professor Wasserstrom made his observation, the trend toward the "reasonableness" rule and its rhetoric has gathered momentum. For example, in Florida v. Jimeno, 111 S.Ct. 1801 (1991), Chief Justice Rehnquist, writing for seven members of the Court, observed that "[t]he touchstone of the Fourth Amendment is reasonableness. . . . The Fourth Amendment does not proscribe all state–initiated searches and seizures; it merely proscribes those which are unreasonable."

In a concurring opinion in California v. Acevedo, 111 S.Ct. 1982 (1991), Justice Scalia described as illusory the apparent victory in the 1960s of the warrant–requirement rule. He observed that "the 'warrant requirement' [has] become so riddled with exceptions that it [is] basically unrecognizable." The Justice called on the other members of the Court, once and for all, to provide clarity in the field by applying exclusively the "reasonableness" rule. Under his interpretation of the Fourth Amendment, a warrant is only required, *i.e.*, its absence is unreasonable, in those cases in which the common law required judicial authorization, and, perhaps, if "changes in the surrounding legal rules . . . [have made] a warrant indispensable to reasonableness where it was once was not."

§ 51 "Neutral and Detached Magistrate"

Page 107, add at the end of footnote 42:

[42] . . . Unfortunately, a common perception among prosecutors, public defenders, and judges is that a significant number of magistrates "knowingly accept police perjury as truthful," in part because they wish to assist the police in the investigation, and in part in order to improve their election chances. Orfield, *Deterrence, Perjury, and the Heater Factor: An Exclusionary Rule in the Chicago Criminal Courts*, 63 U. Colo. L. Rev. 75, 83 (1992) (study of Cook County criminal justice system).

CHAPTER 11

ARRESTS

§ 57   Arrests: Constitutional Law Overview

Page 116, add to footnote 11:

[11] . . . *See also* United States v. Alvarez–Machain, 112 S.Ct. 2188 (1992) (the fact that *D*, a Mexican citizen, was kidnapped with the aid of U.S. drug agents does not prohibit his trial in a U.S. court, for violation of U.S. criminal laws, if the abduction was not in violation of the terms of an extradition treaty).

§ 60   Scope of the *Payton* Rule

Page 119, line 8 from the bottom, add new footnote 23.1:

And, although lower courts . . . without entering the house.[23.1]

[23.1] *E.g.*, United States v. Berkowitz, 927 F.2d 1376, 1386 (7th Cir.), *cert. denied*, 112 S.Ct. 141 (1991) ("*Payton* prohibits only a warrantless *entry* into the home, not a policeman's use of his voice to convey a message of arrest from outside the home") (on this basis, the court held that if the police come to a home without a warrant, knock at the door, *D* opens the door, the officer announces from outside the home that *D* is under arrest, and *D* acquiesces to the arrest, *Payton* is not violated; but if the officer enters before the arrest is made, *Payton* is violated).

CHAPTER 13

SEARCHES INCIDENT TO LAWFUL ARRESTS

§ 68 Prerequisites to the Use of the Warrant Exception

Page 133, add to footnote 11:

[11] . . . *See also* United States v. Alvarez-Machain, 112 S.Ct. 2188 (1992) (the fact that *D*, a Mexican citizen, was kidnapped with the aid of U.S. drug agents does not prohibit his trial in a U.S. court, for violation of U.S. criminal laws, if the abduction did not violate the terms of an extradition treaty).

§ 72 *New York v. Belton*: Bright Lines for Automobiles

Page 141, add at the end of footnote 41:

[41] . . . Other states have also rejected *Belton* in favor of a narrower warrant exception. *E.g.*, State v. Brown, 63 Ohio St.3d 349, 588 N.E.2d 113 (1992) (the police may not open a closed container after the vehicle occupant is under control in the police car); State v. Stroud, 106 Wash.2d 144, 720 P.2d 436 (1986) (plurality opinion) (the police may not search locked containers, including glove compartments, as an incident to a lawful arrest).

§ 74 Pretextual Police Conduct

Page 144, add to footnote 57:

[57] . . . Butterfoss, *Solving the Pretext Puzzle: The Importance of Ulterior Motives and Fabrications in the Supreme Court's Fourth Amendment Pretext Doctrine*, 79 Ky. L.J. 1 (1990).

CHAPTER 14

SEARCHES OF CARS AND CONTAINERS THEREIN

§ 75   Automobile Search–Warrant Exception: General Rules

Page 148, add to footnote 10:

[10] . . . State v. Colvin, 123 N.J. 428, 587 A.2d 1278 (1991) (a warrantless search of an unoccupied parked vehicle is permissible, as long as there is probable cause to search and it is impracticable to secure a warrant) (in the case, the car was unexpectedly discovered, the driver was under arrest, but the police had reason to believe that others would soon remove the contraband from the vehicle).

§ 79   Special Problem: Search of Containers in Cars

Page 153, line 4, add new footnote 31.1:

Courts generally agree . . . the car searched.[31.1]

[31.1] However, occasionally the police have probable cause to search only one portion of a car, such as the trunk, in which case the right to conduct a warrantless search extends only to that area. For example, in California v. Acevedo, 111 S.Ct. 1982 (1991), the police saw *D* place a paper bag, which they had probable cause to believe contained drugs, in the trunk of an automobile. The officers had no reason to believe that contraband was hidden elsewhere in the car. The Court observed that the right to conduct the warrantless search extended only to the trunk.

Page 153, add the following to the citation in footnote 34:

[34] . . . *overruled on other grounds*, California v. Acevedo, 111 S.Ct. 1982 (1991).

Pages 154–155, delete the text to subsection [C][1], and substitute the following text and footnote:

[1]   Overview

Until recently, some closed containers found in cars stopped on the highway constitutionally could be opened without a warrant, whereas others could not be.

The Court originally devised two "container–in–car" rules. One rule, explained in subsection [2] of the Main Volume, which may be coined the "container–coincidentally–in–a–car" rule, provided that if the police have probable cause to search a container before it is placed in a car, a warrant ordinarily is required to open the container, even if it is discovered during an otherwise lawful warrantless car search.

This rule is distinguishable from a second line of cases, the "car–with–a–coincidental–container" line, considered in subsection [3] of the Main Volume. This line holds that if, while the police are conducting a lawful car search, they coincidentally come across a container, their right to search the car without a warrant extends to the container, as long as the container is large enough to hold the object of the search.

In *California v. Acevedo*,[39.1] the Court concluded that these two lines of cases were unduly confusing, led to anomalous results, and were unnecessary to protect legitimate privacy interests. Therefore, it abandoned the first line of cases: hereafter, any container found during a lawful "automobile exception" search, may be opened and searched without a warrant, as long as it is large enough to conceal the object of the search.

In view of *Acevedo*, the distinctions described in the Main Volume are now legally irrelevant. However, the previous lines of cases must be understood in order to evaluate the wisdom and significance of *Acevedo*. Furthermore, "search" law regarding containers seized from sites other than motor vehicles remains presently untouched by the decision.

[39.1] 111 S.Ct. 1982 (1991).

Page 156, add the following to the citation in footnote 43:

[43] . . . *overruled in* California v. Acevedo, 111 S.Ct. 1982 (1991). *See* § 79[C][5] (Pock. Pt.) *infra*.

Page 158, add to footnote 50:

[50] . . . However, as explained in new subsection [5], *infra*, the Court in *Acevedo* overruled Arkansas v. Sanders and abandoned the *Chadwick-Sanders* rule. Therefore, the assumption that both "container-in-car" rules still apply is no longer appropriate. Nonetheless, it is useful to consider the following examples, in order to see how slender the distinctions were before *Acevedo*. The likely post–*Acevedo* outcomes in the following examples are set out in new footnote 61, *infra*.

Page 160, at the end of the chapter, add the following new subsection:

[5] *California v. Acevedo*: Seeking Clarity

In *California v. Acevedo*,[55] the Supreme Court erased the "curious line between the search of an automobile that coincidentally turns up a container [*Ross*] and the search of a container that coincidentally turns up in an automobile [*Chadwick–Sanders*]." Stating that "[t]he protections of the Fourth Amendment must not turn on such coincidences," a six–Justice majority overruled *Sanders*, abandoned the latter line of container cases, and held that any container found in a car during an otherwise lawful "automobile exception" search may be opened without a warrant (if it is large enough to contain the object of the search), whether or not there is probable cause to search elsewhere in the car.

In *Acevedo*, as police looked on, *D* left a residence holding a closed paper bag that the officers had probable cause to believe contained illegal narcotics, placed

[55] 111 S.Ct. 1982 (1991).

it in the trunk of a car, and drove away. Fearing the loss of the contraband, the police stopped the car on the road, opened the trunk, and inspected the contents of the bag, which contained marijuana.

Thus, the case was similar to *Chadwick* and *Sanders* in a key respect: the police had probable cause to search a specific container before it was placed in the car. Moreover, as in *Sanders*, the container was not searched until the car was on the highway. The case was unlike *Ross* in an important respect: in *Ross* the police had probable cause to search a car trunk for contraband, during which search they unexpectedly discovered a closed paper bag; in *Acevedo*, probable cause to search did not extend beyond the closed paper bag.[56]

Justice Blackmun, author of dissenting opinions in *Chadwick* and *Sanders*, wrote the majority opinion in *Acevedo*. In defense of the change in the law, he argued, first, that "[t]he discrepancy between the two rules has led to confusion for law enforcement officers," rather than to provide "clear and unequivocal" guidelines.

Second, because the line between probable cause to search a car and probable cause to search a container in the car is not always bright, "separate rules . . . may enable the police to broaden their power to make warrantless searches and disserve privacy interests." Justice Blackmun worried that "if the police know they may open a bag only if they are actually searching the entire car, they may search more extensively than they otherwise would in order to establish the general probable cause required by *Ross*."

Third, the majority maintained, "[t]o the extent that the *Chadwick–Sanders* rule protects privacy, its protection is minimal." The police may already lawfully open many containers found in cars without a warrant: for example, if the police have probable cause to believe that a container in a car holds criminal evidence, the same probable cause will often justify an arrest of the occupant, at which time the container, if it is in the passenger compartment, may be opened incident to the arrest.[57] Furthermore, even under the *Chadwick* rule, the police are allowed to seize a container found in a car without a warrant and hold it until they obtain judicial authorization to open it, which the Court assumed would occur in the great majority of cases.

Fourth, the conjunction of the two rules results in an anomaly: the more likely the police are to discover drugs in a container, the less authority they have to search it. That is, under *Ross*, the police may conduct a warrantless search of a container

---

[56] Contrary to the remarks in the text, the Court in *Acevedo* stated that "[t]he facts in this case closely resemble the facts in *Ross*. In *Ross*, the police had probable cause to believe that drugs were stored in the trunk of a particular car. . . . Furthermore, for what it is worth, in *Ross*, as here, the drugs in the trunk were contained in a brown paper bag."

The first "resemblance" omits the key dissimilarity, which represents the issue in this case, namely, that the police in *Ross* had probable cause to search the trunk, whereas in *Acevedo* the probable cause focused on the trunk only because it contained the paper bag. As for the second similarity ("for what it is worth"), it is worth nothing as long as the Court continues to hold, as it did in *Ross, see* § 79[B] *supra*, that closed paper bags (of any color) are as worthy of Fourth Amendment protection as other containers.

[57] New York v. Belton, 453 U.S. 454, *reh'g denied*, 453 U.S. 950 (1981). *See* § 72 *supra*.

coincidentally found during a car search, *i.e.*, a container that they have no particular reason to believe contains contraband; but, if they have probable cause to search the container, and no basis for searching the rest of the car, *Chadwick–Sanders* requires a warrant to open the container.

Justice Stevens, author of *Ross*, dissented in *Acevedo*.[58] He disagreed with the majority's claim that the existing law was confusing.[59] Second, and more significantly, he found "puzzling" the majority's suggestion that, under the old rule, the police might search an entire car in order to justify a *Ross* search:

> I assume that the Court does not mean to suggest that evidence found during the course of a search may provide the probable cause that justifies the search. Our cases have unequivocally rejected this bootstrap justification for a search which was not lawful when it commenced.

Third, he disagreed with the majority's claim that the privacy interests at stake in the car–container cases are minimal. As he pointed out, the paper bag opened in this case would not have fallen within the search–incident–to–a–lawful–arrest rule, as it was found in the trunk rather than in the passenger portion of the car. According to Justice Stevens, the privacy effect of the Court's ruling is substantial: "the privacy interest that protects the contents of a [container] . . . [now] simply vanishes when its owner climbs into a [vehicle]." In contrast, under the *Chadwick–Sanders* rule, "the decision to invade the privacy of an individual's personal effects . . . [would be] made by a neutral magistrate rather than an agent of the Executive."

Fourth, Justice Stevens denied that the two lines of cases resulted in an anomaly unless, as he explained:

> one accepts the flawed premise that the degree to which the police are likely to discover contraband is correlated with their authority to search *without a warrant*. Yet, even proof beyond a reasonable doubt will not justify a warrantless search that is not supported by one of the exceptions to the warrant requirement.

Moreover, the dissent suggested, the majority's cure for the "anomaly" causes a new one. After *Acevedo*, if a person carries a container with him on a public street, *Chadwick* still applies, *i.e.*, the police must secure a warrant. But, the police may open the container without a warrant (assuming probable cause) as soon as it is placed in the more–private confines of a locked car trunk. Yet, the person's privacy interest in the contents of the container is the same; nor is there any reason to distinguish on the grounds of mobility, because the container may be seized on the street or from the car without a warrant, and held until a magistrate can make a probable–cause determination.

The Court overruled *Sanders*, but what remains of *Chadwick*? The majority does not openly question that opinion's basic premise that a person has a legitimate

---

[58] Justice Marshall joined in the dissent. Justice White separately dissented, stating that he agreed with most of Justice Stevens' remarks.

[59] However, as demonstrated in subsection [4] *supra*, the line between the two sets of cases was quite thin.

expectation of privacy in closed containers, outside the context of a vehicle.**60** However, what if, as in *Chadwick*, the police conduct the warrantless search the moment the container is placed in the car, but before it is taken onto the highway? *Acevedo*'s reasoning suggests that such a search now falls within the general "automobile search" exception to the warrant requirement. Language in the opinion supports this conclusion: according to Justice Blackmun, "*Ross* now applies to all searches of containers found in an automobile."

Apparently, the only reason *Chadwick* remains good law regarding containers found in cars is that (as *Acevedo* pointed out) the government in that case did not seek to justify the search on the basis of the automobile exception, but rather argued on the ground that movable luggage is analogous to an automobile. If a case like *Chadwick* arises again, and the government asserts the automobile exception to the warrant requirement, the Court should permit the search on the basis of *Ross-Acevedo*.**61**

---

60 *E.g.*, U.S. v. $639,558 in United States Currency, 955 F.2d 712 (D.C. Cir. 1992) (ruling that the holding of *Chadwick* survives *Acevedo* and, therefore, a warrantless search of a closed container, seized from *D*'s "sleeper" compartment on a train, is unconstitutional).

However, Justice Scalia is on record in *Acevedo* in favor of overruling *Chadwick*. He would hold that a warrantless search of any closed container discovered outside a privately owned building, if founded upon probable cause, is permissible.

61 In view of *Acevedo*, the *Ross* doctrine clearly applies in Examples 2 through 5, considered in subsection [4], *supra*. In Example 1, *Chadwick* seemingly still applies to the container searched before it was put in the vehicle. However, once the container is placed in the car (as hypothesized in the second paragraph of Example 1), *Ross-Acevedo* should apply.

CHAPTER 15

THE "PLAIN VIEW" DOCTRINE

§ 80   General Principles

Page 161, add at the end of footnote 1:

[1] . . . The related topics of "plain smell," "plain touch" and "plain hearing" are considered in 1 W. LaFave at § 2.2(a); *see also* Holtz, *The "Plain Touch" Corollary: A Natural and Foreseeable Consequence of the Plain View Doctrine*, 95 Dick. L. Rev. 521 (1991).

§ 82   Application of the Plain–View Doctrine: *Arizona v. Hicks*

Page 165, line 6 from the bottom of the page, add new footnote 15.1:

Nor is a . . . a short distance.[15.1]

[15.1] *See also* Cloutier, *Arizona v. Hicks: The Failure to Recognize Limited Inspections as Reasonable in Fourth Amendment Jurisprudence*, 24 Colum. J.L. & Soc. Probs. 351 (1991) (contending that *Hicks* should be overruled, and that limited plain-view inspections should be allowed on the basis of reasonable suspicion).

CHAPTER 16

INVENTORY SEARCHES

§ 84 Automobile Inventories: General Principles

Page 169, add to footnote 1:

[1] . . . LaFave, *Controlling Discretion by Administrative Regulations: The Use, Misuse, and Nonuse of Police Rules and Policies in Fourth Amendment Adjudication*, 89 Mich. L. Rev. 442 (1990) (especially pp. 447–463).

§ 87 Arrest Inventories

Page 175, line 7, add new footnote 29.1:

The Court stated . . . into the jail.[29.1]

[29.1] . . . *But see* State v. Perham, 814 P.2d 914 (Haw. 1991) (under the state constitution, it was impermissible for the police to open and search the contents of *D*'s wallet as part of an arrest inventory, in absence of evidence that such an exploratory search was the least intrusive means of accomplishing the purposes of safeguarding the property and of protecting the police against fraudulent claims).

CHAPTER 17

CONSENT TO SEARCH

§ 89 The Nature of Lawful Consent: General Principles

Page 179, add the following new subsection at the bottom of the page:

[D] Scope of Consent

As mentioned at the end of the preceding subsection, a warrantless "consent" search is invalid if the officer exceeds the scope of the consent granted. A consent search, however, is virtually never negotiated like a contract, so it is often unclear how extensively the police may search based on the permission given.

In *Florida v. Jimeno*,[18.1] the Supreme Court provided its clearest guidance to date on the "scope of consent" issue. In *Jimeno*, an officer stopped *D*'s car on the highway in order to issue a traffic citation. Because he had reason to suspect that *D* was carrying narcotics in the car, the officer requested permission to search the vehicle for narcotics. *D* consented. During the search, the officer opened a folded paper bag, in which he discovered a kilogram of cocaine. The trial court suppressed the evidence on the ground that *D* had not expressly consented to a search of the container. The Supreme Court reversed.

Chief Justice Rehnquist declared that "[t]he standard for measuring the scope of a suspect's consent . . . is that of 'objective' reasonableness — what would the typical reasonable person have understood by the exchange between the officer and the suspect?" On the basis of the facts here, the Court maintained that "it was objectively reasonable for the police to conclude that the general consent to search [*D*'s] car included consent to search containers within that car which might bear drugs." In other words, regardless of whether *D* subjectively considered the container when he gave the officer consent to search, the officer acted reasonably in interpreting *D*'s consent to include the right to open the folded paper bag, in view of the fact that D did not explicitly limit the scope of the search.

Jimeno does *not* stand for the broad proposition that the police may, in the absence of an expressed limitation, open every container discovered during a consent search. According to the Court, "[t]he scope of a search is generally defined by its expressed object." Therefore, it would be improper for the police to open a container too small to hide the object of the search.

[18.1] 111 S.Ct. 1801 (1991).

Potentially more significantly, the Court in dictum distinguished the present case from one in which the police, pursuant to consent to search a car trunk, break open a locked suitcase found in the trunk. In the latter situation, the Court opined, "[i]t is very likely unreasonable to think that a suspect, by consent to the search of his trunk, has agreed to the breaking open of [the suitcase]. . . ." However, as the dissent pointed out, this distinction is questionable in view of prior case law,[18.2] which suggests that closed paper bags are as worthy of Fourth Amendment protection as locked suitcases.

[18.2] *See* § 79[B] *supra.*

§ 91   Third-Party Consent

Page 183, add at the end of footnote 34:

[34] . . . *See also* In re D.A.G., 484 N.W.2d 787 (Mn. 1992) (under the state constitution, a present joint occupant's right to be free from the warrantless search of a premises prevails over an absent joint occupant's right to consent to that search).

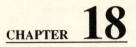
MINIMALLY INTRUSIVE SEARCHES AND SEIZURES: THE *TERRY* PRINCIPLE

§ 95 "Reasonable Suspicion"

Page 189, add at the end of footnote 20:

[20] . . . Is one "common sense conclusion about human behavior" that one who flees upon observing a police officer is guilty of criminal conduct or, at least, of planned criminal wrongdoing? In California v. Hodari D., 111 S.Ct. 1547 (1991), Justice Scalia, writing for seven justices, hinted in dictum that unprovoked flight constitutes reasonable suspicion to stop the fleeing party: "That it would be unreasonable to stop, for brief inquiry, young men who scatter in panic upon the mere sighting of the police is not self–evident, and arguably contradicts proverbial common sense. *See Proverbs* 28:1 ('The wicked flee when no man pursueth')."

Justices Stevens and Marshall disapproved of the "gratuitous" Biblical quotation, which "mistakenly assumes that innocent residents have no reason to fear the sudden approach of strangers. We have previously considered, and rejected, this ivory–towered analysis of the real world for it fails to describe the experience of many residents, particularly if they are members of a minority." Quoting Alberty v. United States, 162 U.S. 499 (1896), the dissent warned that innocent people sometimes flee "from the scene of a crime through fear of being apprehended as the guilty parties, or from an unwillingness to appear as witnesses." Although the dissenters did not say so, some people, especially racial minorities, might also flee because they fear physical mistreatment by the police.

Page 191, add to footnote 31:

[31] . . . *See generally* Rudstein, *White on White: Anonymous Tips, Reasonable Suspicion, and the Constitution*, 79 Ky. L.J. 661 (1991).

§ 102 Suspicionless *Terry*–Level Seizures

Page 202, add to footnote 78:

[78] . . . LaFave, *Controlling Discretion by Administrative Regulations: The Use, Misuse, and Nonuse of Police Rules and Policies in Fourth Amendment Adjudication*, 89 Mich. L. Rev. 442 (1990); Strossen, *Michigan Department of State Police v. Sitz: A Roadblock to Meaningful Enforcement of Constitutional Rights*, 42 Hastings L.J. 185 (1991).

Page 205, line 6, add new footnote 85:

He accused the . . . by the Constitution."[85]

[85] Upon remand to the Court of Appeals of Michigan, that court held that the sobriety checkpoint set up in *Sitz* violated the Michigan constitution. Sitz v. Michigan Dept. of State Police, 193 Mich. App. 690, 485 N.W.2d 135 (1992). *See also* State v. Sims, 808 P.2d 141 (Utah Ct. App. 1991) (under the state constitution, the police may not conduct a suspicionless highway roadblock unless and until the state legislature authorizes the practice).

CHAPTER **19**

"SPECIAL GOVERNMENTAL NEED" (FORMERLY, "ADMINISTRATIVE") SEARCHES

§ 103   "Special Governmental Needs" Exception: In General

Page 207, add to footnote 1:

[1] . . . Mussio, *Drawing the Line Between Administrative and Criminal Searches: Defining the "Object of the Search" in Environmental Inspections*, 18 B.C. Envtl. Aff. L. Rev. 185 (1990); Reamey, *When "Special Needs" Meet Probable Cause: Denying the Devil Benefit of Law*, 19 Hastings Const. L.Q. 295 (1992); Stuntz, *Implicit Bargains, Government Power, and the Fourth Amendment*, 44 Stan. L. Rev. 553 (1992).

§ 104   Administrative–Code Searches

Page 208, add to footnote 8:

[8] . . . LaFave, *Controlling Discretion by Administrative Regulations: The Use, Misuse, and Nonuse of Police Rules and Policies in Fourth Amendment Adjudication*, 89 Mich. L. Rev. 442 (1990); Mussio, n. 1 (Pock. Pt.) *supra*.

CHAPTER **20**

FOURTH AMENDMENT: "STANDING"

§ 116   What Has *Rakas* Wrought?: An Analysis

Page 230, line 8, add new footnote 47.1:

Indeed, in view . . . automobile is significant.[47.1]

[47.1] However, the Court in *Rakas* expressly left open the issue of whether "the same expectations of privacy are warranted in a car as would be justified in a dwelling house in analogous circumstances." *Rakas*, 439 U.S. at 148. Thus, the Court could ultimately hold that its analysis in *Olson* regarding standing to contest a search of a home does not apply to searches of automobiles. Just as a person is said to have a lesser expectation of privacy in an automobile than in a home, *see* § 78 *supra*, it is possible that a person is entitled to contest a search of a home under less stringent circumstances than to contest a search of a car.

(Matthew Bender & Co., Inc.)
(Pub. 791)

CHAPTER 21

FOURTH AMENDMENT: EXCLUSIONARY RULE

§ 117   Development of the Exclusionary Rule

Page 235, add at the end of footnote 2:

[2] . . . For an examination of the exclusionary rule under Canada's Charter of Rights, see McDonald, *The Exclusion of Evidence Obtained by Constitutionally Impermissible Means in Canada*, 9 Crim. Just. Ethics (Summer/Fall 1990), at 43.

§ 120   Exclusionary Rule: Is It a Good Idea?

Page 241, add to footnote 33:

[33] . . . Dripps, *Beyond the Warren Court and Its Conservative Critics: Toward a Unified Theory of Constitutional Criminal Procedure*, 23 U. Mich. J.L. Ref. 591 (1990); Heffernan & Lovely, *Evaluating the Fourth Amendment Exclusionary Rule: The Problem of Police Compliance with the Law*, 24 U. Mich. J.L. Ref. 311 (1991); Orfield, *Deterrence, Perjury, and the Heater Factor: An Exclusionary Rule in the Chicago Criminal Courts*, 63 U. Colo. L. Rev. 75 (1992); Stuntz, *Warrants and Fourth Amendment Remedies*, 77 Va. L. Rev. 881 (1991).

Page 241, line 4 from the bottom, add new footnote 37.1:

Most violations of . . . court does subsequently.[37.1]

[37.1] . . . *See* Heffernan & Lovely, n. 33 (Pock. Pt.) *supra*, at 332–45 (finding that even well–trained officers are mistaken about Fourth Amendment law approximately 25% of the time).

Page 242, add at the end of footnote 39:

[39] . . . *See also* Orfield, n. 33 (Pock. Pt.) *supra*, at 82–83 (in a study of Cook County, Illinois criminal courts, the author discovered "pervasive police perjury," including "systematic fabrications in case reports and affidavits for search warrants, creating artificial probable cause").

Page 243, add at the end of footnote 49:

[49] . . . *See also* Orfield, n. 33 (Pock. Pt.) *supra*, at 80, 94–95 (in a study of Cook County, Illinois criminal courts, the author found that the exclusionary rule had an "institutional deterrent effect," in that "police administrators and prosecutors respond to the loss of evidence by designing programs and procedures to ensure better compliance with the Fourth Amendment.").

Page 245, add to footnote 61:

[61] . . . *See also* Uchida & Bynum, *Search Warrants, Motions to Suppress and "Lost Cases": The Effectiveness of the Exclusionary Rule in Seven Jurisdictions*, 81 J. Crim. L. & Criminology 1034 (1991) (study of seven cities found that in cases involving search warrants, motions to suppress were successful in only 0.9% of the cases; in terms of defendants, judges sustained motions of 2% of all defendants; 1.5% of the defendants were set free based on successful motions to suppress).

Page 246, end of subsection [C], add new footnote 67.1:

Therefore, just as . . . an individual case.[67.1]

[67.1] *See* Heffernan & Lovely, n. 33 (Pock. Pt.) *supra*, at 369 (arguing that once officers receive extensive training in the law, they are correct about the law more often that they are not, and in view of this success, "there is no reason to concede defeat [as to deterrence] as far as the rules of search and seizure are concerned.").

§ 121 Limitations On The Scope of the Exclusionary Rule

Page 248, add at the end of footnote 84:

[84] . . . United States v. McCrory, 930 F.2d 63 (D.C. Cir. 1991), *cert denied*, 112 S.Ct. 885 (1992) (evidence seized in violation of the Fourth Amendment may be considered by the judge in determining the defendant's appropriate sentence under the federal sentencing guidelines).

§ 122 The *Leon* "Good Faith" Exception: General Principles

Page 249, add to footnote 92:

[92] . . . Note, *Errors in Good Faith: The Leon Exception Six Years Later*, 89 Mich. L. Rev. 625 (1990).

Page 251, add at the end of footnote 98:

[98] . . . *But see* United States v. Decker, 956 F.2d 773 (8th. Cir. 1992) (holding that the good–faith rule does not apply to a warrant signed by a magistrate who never read it; the court ruled that under such circumstances the judge has acted as a "rubber stamp" for the police; the court explicitly rejected the government's argument that, in view of the Court's citation to *Lo-Ji Sales* in *Leon*, this exception to *Leon* does not apply unless the issuing magistrate is a participant in the search).

§ 124 The Long–Term Implications of *Leon*

Page 254, add at the end of footnote 113:

[113] . . . Applying their state constitutions, Pennsylvania and Vermont courts have also rejected the *Leon* exception to the Fourth Amendment exclusionary rule. Commonwealth v. Edmunds, 526 Pa. 374, 586 A.2d 887 (1991); State v. Oakes, 598 A.2d 119 (Vt. 1991).

Page 255, add at the end of footnote 119:

[119] . . . However, the Fifth Circuit of the United States Court of Appeals purports to recognize a *Leon*–like exception in cases involving warrantless arrests and investigatory stops. United States v. de Leon–Reyna, 930 F.2d 396 (5th Cir. 1991); *see* United States v. Williams, 622 F.2d 830 (5th Cir. 1980), *cert. denied*, 449 U.S. 1127 (1981).

§ 125   "Fruit of the Poisonous Tree" Doctrine

Page 257, add at the end of footnote 129:

[129] . . . *See generally* Bradley, *Murray v. United States: The Bell Tolls for the Search Warrant Requirement*, 64 Ind. L.J. 907 (1989).

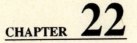

INTERROGATION LAW: OVERVIEW

§ 128   Interrogation Law: The Policy Debate

Page 265, add to footnote 12:

[12] . . . Berger, *Legislating Confession Law in Great Britain: A Statutory Approach to Police Interrogations*, 24 U. Mich. J.L. Ref. 1 (1990).

CHAPTER 23

COERCED ("INVOLUNTARY") CONFESSIONS

§ 130 "Involuntariness": General Constitutional Rule

Page 272, add at the end of footnote 19:

[19] . . . The Supreme Court answered affirmatively the question raised in the appeal. Arizona v. Fulminante, 111 S.Ct. 1246, *reh'g denied*, 111 S.Ct. 2067 (1991); *see generally* Ogletree, *Arizona v. Fulminante: The Harm of Applying Harmless Error to Coerced Confessions*, 105 Harv. L. Rev. 152 (1991). Notwithstanding *Payne* and other cases that indicated that a conviction must automatically be overturned if the defendant's coerced confession was erroneously introduced at her trial, five justices in *Fulminante* ruled that the usual harmless–error rule applies in such cases, *i.e.*, a conviction need not be overturned because of the erroneous admission of a coerced confession, if the prosecutor proves beyond a reasonable doubt that its admission did not prejudice the outcome of the trial. *See* § 13 *supra*.

However, five members of the Court (Justices White, Marshall, Blackmun, Stevens, and, Kennedy) warned that appellate courts ought to treat skeptically any claim that a coerced confession did not prejudice the defendant's ability to obtain a fair trial. According to Justice White, "[a] confession is like no other evidence," in that juries have great difficulty putting a confession aside in order to look for corroborating evidence of guilt. He warned that "a full confession in which the defendant discloses the motive for and means of the crime may tempt the jury to rely upon that evidence alone in reaching its decision." As well, Justice Kennedy stated in a separate opinion that "the court conducting a harmless–error inquiry must appreciate the indelible impact a full confession may have on the trier of fact."

§ 133 "Voluntariness": Totality–of–the–Circumstances Test

Page 276, add at the end of footnote 50:

[50] . . . *See* Arizona v. Fulminante, 111 S.Ct. 1246, *reh'g denied*, 111 S.Ct. 2067 (1991) (threat of physical force by a private person, if exploited by a state agent, may render a confession involuntary) (in the case, *D*, a prison inmate, was physically threatened by fellow prisoners because of a rumor that he was suspected of an unsolved child murder; *X*, a fellow inmate who was also a paid government informant, offered to protect *D* from violence in exchange for the truth about the crime; *D* confessed; describing the question as a close one, the Court held that the confession was involuntary).

§ 135 Scope of the Coerced–Confession Exclusionary Rule

Page 278, line 3 from the bottom of the text, add new footnote 64.1:

The Supreme Court . . . that it does.[64.1]

[64.1] The Court implied as much in Oregon v. Elstad, 470 U.S. 298 (1985). *Elstad* involved the question of whether the fruit–of–the–poisonous–tree doctrine applies to violations of the rules announced in Miranda v. Arizona, 384 U.S. 436 (1966). The Court stated that exclusion of evidence under the "fruit" doctrine "assumes the existence of a constitutional violation." Because a violation of the *Miranda* doctrine is a violation of a non–constitutional rule intended to deter coerced confessions, *see* § 141 *infra*, the "fruit" rule does not generally apply to *Miranda* violations. *See* § 147[C][3] *infra*. By negative implication, the fruit–of–the–poisonous–tree doctrine *does* apply to confessions unconstitutionally coerced.

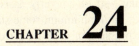

CHAPTER **24**

MIRANDA v. ARIZONA

§ 142 Meaning of *Miranda*: "Custody"

Page 295, at the beginning of § 142, add the following new "bibliography" footnote 73.1:

[73.1] *See generally* Yeager, *Rethinking Custodial Interrogation*, 28 Am. Crim. L. Rev. 1 (1990).

§ 143 Meaning of *Miranda*: "Interrogation"

Page 297, add to footnote 84:

[84] . . . Yeager, n. 73.1 *supra.*

Page 300, add at the end of footnote 95:

[95] . . . This response was admissible, however, despite the absence of *Miranda* warnings, because *D*'s response – accurately counting aloud – was not incriminating except in so far as his speech was slurred. As for the incriminating nature of *D*'s slurred speech, this constituted "nontestimonial components" of his response. *See* § 163[A] of the text (including the discussion of *Muniz* at § 163[A][3]).

§ 145 Waiver of *Miranda* Rights

Page 305, add at the end of footnote 115:

[115] . . . *See* McNeil v. Wisconsin, 111 S.Ct. 2204, 2208 (1991) ("The *Edwards* rule, moreover, is *not* offense–specific: once a suspect invokes the *Miranda* right to counsel for interrogation regarding one offense, he may not be reapproached regarding *any* offense unless counsel is present.").

Page 307, immediately preceding § 146, add the following new subsection:

[e] When *Edwards* Does Not Apply

Not all requests to consult with an attorney trigger the *Edwards* rule. In *McNeil v. Wisconsin,*[125.1] the Court stated:

[125.1] 111 S.Ct. 2204 (1991).

The rule of that case [*Edwards*] applies only when the suspect "ha[s] *expressed*" his wish for the particular sort of lawyerly assistance that is the subject of *Miranda*. . . . It requires, at a minimum, some statement that can reasonably be construed to be an expression of a desire for the assistance of an attorney *in dealing with custodial interrogation by the police.*

For example, in *McNeil*, D invoked his right to counsel at a bail hearing – a judicial proceeding – rather than during or immediately preceding custodial police interrogation. The Court held that the *Miranda–Edwards* cease–interrogation rule did not apply in these circumstances, *i.e.*, his statement could not "reasonably be construed to be an expression of a desire for the assistance of an attorney in dealing with custodial interrogation by the police." By requesting a lawyer when he did, D invoked his *Sixth* Amendment right to counsel, which differs in key respects from the Fifth Amendment–*Miranda* version of the right that is the basis of the *Edwards* rule.[125.2]

Second, the *McNeil* Court expressed doubt that the *Miranda* right to counsel can ever be invoked "anticipatorily." That is, the Court stated, "[m]ost rights must be asserted when the government seeks to take the actions they protect against." Therefore, without deciding the issue, the Court hinted that an assertion of the *Miranda–Edwards* right to consult with counsel is not effective, no matter how explicit the request, if it is "asserted initially outside the context of custodial interrogation," such as at a judicial proceeding.

[125.2] For a comparison of the Fifth and Sixth Amendment rights to counsel, *see generally* § 156 *infra*.

CHAPTER 25

INTERROGATION LAW: SIXTH AMENDMENT RIGHT TO COUNSEL

§ 149   *Massiah v. United States*

Page 314, add to footnote 9:

⁹ . . . Office of Legal Policy, U.S. Dep't of Justice, Truth in Criminal Justice Series, Report No. 3, Report to the Attorney General on the Sixth Amendment Right to Counsel Under the *Massiah* Line of Cases, *reprinted in* 22 U. Mich. J.L. Ref. 661 (1989); Tomkovicz, *The Truth About Massiah*, 23 U. Mich. J.L. Ref. 641 (1990); Comment, *The Sixth Amendment as Constitutional Theory: Does Originalism Require that Massiah Be Abandoned?*, 82 J. Crim. L. & Criminology 423 (1991).

§ 153   Waiver of the Right to Counsel

Page 325, line 13 from the top of the page, add new footnote 55.1:

In *Michigan v. Jackson*, . . . with the government.⁵⁵·¹

⁵⁵·¹ However, because the Sixth Amendment right to counsel is offense–specific, *see* § 155[C] *infra*, the *Jackson* cease–interrogation rule does not apply, even after a suspect invokes her request for an attorney, to crimes for which the defendant has not yet been formally charged. *See* McNeil v. Wisconsin, 111 S.Ct. 2204 (1991) (*D* invoked his Sixth Amendment right to counsel regarding an armed robbery, for which the right had attached; the police were not required under *Jackson* to cease interrogation regarding other, uncharged offenses).

§ 155   Scope of the Sixth Amendment Exclusionary Rule

Page 329, line 6 from the bottom of the page, add new footnote 69.1:

Although the right . . . statements were elicited.⁶⁹·¹

⁶⁹·¹ *See* McNeil v. Wisconsin, 111 S.Ct. 2204, 2207 (1991) ("The Sixth Amendment right [to counsel], however, is offense–specific.").

   (Pub. 791)

§ 156   Right–to–Counsel Summary: Sixth Amendment versus *Miranda*

Page 331, add at the end of footnote 82:

[82] . . . *See* McNeil v. Wisconsin, 111 S.Ct. 2204, 2209 (1991) (stating that the two versions of the right to counsel "protect . . . quite different interest[s]," and that the Sixth Amendment right is both narrower and broader than the Fifth Amendment right).

Page 332, add the following new text at the end of the page:

6. A defendant may assert her Sixth Amendment right to counsel, so as to bar police questioning, during a judicial proceeding or while in police custody preceding or during the interrogation. However, it is questionable whether a suspect may initially invoke her Fifth Amendment right to counsel at any time other than immediately prior to police custodial interrogation.

7. Waiver principles vary. Once a person asserts her Fifth Amendment right to counsel regarding an offense, she may not be approached regarding any other offense, unless counsel is present; however, because the Sixth Amendment right is offense–specific, invocation of the latter right to counsel does not bar questioning regarding uncharged offenses.

CHAPTER 26

PRIVILEGE AGAINST SELF–INCRIMINATION:
GENERAL PRINCIPLES

§ 159   Is the Privilege a Good Idea?: The Controversy

Page 335, add to footnote 12:

[12] . . . Dripps, *Self-Incrimination and Self-Preservation: A Skeptical View*, 1991 U. Ill. L. Rev. 329; Schulhofer, *Some Kind Words for the Privilege Against Self-Incrimination*, 26 Val. U. L. Rev. 311 (1991); Thomas & Bilder, *Aristotle's Paradox and the Self-Incrimination Puzzle*, 82 J. Crim. L. & Criminology 243 (1991).

§ 160   The Fifth Amendment Privilege: Who Is Protected?

Page 339, add at the end of footnote 49:

[49] . . . *See generally* Rosenberg, *Bouknight: Of Abused Children and the Parental Privilege Against Self–Incrimination*, 76 Iowa L. Rev. 535 (1991).

§ 162   Procedures Relating to the Invocation of the Privilege

Page 341, add at the end of footnote 59:

[59] . . . However, various state courts have declined to follow *Kastigar*'s constitutional lead, and have construed the privilege against self–incrimination contained in their state constitutions to require transactional immunity. *See* State v. Gonzalez, 825 P.2d 920 (Alas.App. 1992); State v. Miyasaki, 62 Haw. 269, 614 P.2d 915 (1980); State v. Soriano, 68 Or.App. 642, 684 P.2d 1220, *aff'd en banc*, 298 Or. 392, 693 P.2d 26 (1984); Attorney General v. Colleton, 387 Mass. 790, 444 N.E.2d 915 (1982); Wright v. McAdory, 536 So.2d 897 (Miss. 1988).

CHAPTER 27

EYEWITNESS IDENTIFICATION PROCEDURES

§ 168 Identification Procedures: Due Process of Law

Page 354, add to footnote 26:

[26] . . . Rosenberg, *Rethinking the Right to Due Process in Connection With Pretrial Identification Procedures: An Appraisal and a Proposal*, 79 Ky. L.J. 259 (1991).

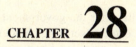

CHAPTER **28**

ENTRAPMENT

§ 171 Entrapment: The Subjective Test

[In some printings of the text] Page 358, second to the last line of the text, add the word "not" after the word "was":

. . . On the other hand, entrapment was *not* proved in *Russell*. . . .

Page 359, immediately preceding subsection [B], add the following new text and footnotes:

The Supreme Court again considered the entrapment defense – in particular, the issue of what constitutes "predisposition" – in *Jacobson v. United States*.[10.1]

The pertinent facts were these: In February, 1984, *D* ordered by mail and received two magazines (*Bare Boys I* and *Bare Boys II*) that contained photographs of nude pre–teen and teenage boys. Receipt of these magazines, which did not depict the youths in sexual activity, was lawful under both federal and state law.

A few months later, Congress passed the Child Protection Act of 1984, which prohibited the receipt by mail of sexually explicit depictions of children. Thereafter, various federal agencies, including the Postal Service and Customs Service, began sophisticated "sting" operations intended to arrest violators of the new law.

D's name came to the government's attention after it obtained the mailing list from the bookstore that sold him the *Bare Boys* magazines. Beginning in January, 1985, government agents sent mail to *D* through five fictitious organizations, such as the "American Hedonist Society." Some of the mailings promoted sexual freedom, expressed opposition to censorship, and called for statutory reform of the laws relating to sexually explicit materials. Two pieces of correspondence included "sexual attitude" surveys purporting to measure the recipient's enjoyment of various sexual materials. *D* responded to the surveys, indicating that he had a moderate level of interest in "pre–teen sex" and "preteen sex–homosexual" materials, but also indicating that he was opposed to pedophilia.

The government also sent *D*, again through a fictitious organization, a bogus list of "pen pals" with similar interests in sexual materials. When *D* failed to initiate correspondence with persons from the list, a government pen pal wrote him instead. *D* answered twice before discontinuing the correspondence. In one letter he stated

---

[10.1] 112 S.Ct. 1535 (1992).

that he enjoyed "male–male items," although at no time did he mention child pornography.

In March 1987, 26 months after the government first targeted *D*, a fictitious organization mailed *D* a brochure advertising photographs of young boys engaged in sex. *D* placed an order that was not filled. Shortly thereafter, *D* ordered a magazine (*Boys Who Love Boys*) from a second government–sponsored catalogue. *D* was arrested upon receipt of the magazine at the Post Office. In a subsequent search of *D*'s home, the government found the *Bare Boys* magazines purchased in 1984 and the materials sent to him from the government, but they discovered nothing else that suggested that *D* purchased or collected child pornography.

At trial, *D* pleaded entrapment. When asked why he purchased the illegal materials, he explained that "[w]ell, the statement was made [in the government correspondence] of all the trouble and the hysteria over pornography and I wanted to see what the material was. It didn't describe the — I didn't know for sure what kind of sexual action they were referring to in the . . . letter." The jury rejected *D*'s entrapment claim.

By a 5–4 vote, the Supreme Court reversed *D*'s conviction. It ruled that as a matter of law the government failed to prove beyond a reasonable doubt (the burden of proof in federal trials, as stated on page 360 of the Main Volume) that *D* "was independently predisposed to commit the crime for which he was arrested."

At one level the Court's ruling seems unsurprising. In view of the length and sophistication of the sting operation, jurors could well have harbored reasonable doubt as to *D*'s predisposition to purchase child pornography. An acquittal, therefore, would not have been startling. But, the Supreme Court functions as an appellate court, not as a jury. Accordingly, reversal of the conviction was only proper if, construing all of the evidence in the light most favorable to the government, no rational jury could have concluded beyond a reasonable doubt that *D* was predisposed.

Why was there insufficient evidence of predisposition to convict? The Court, per Justice White, stated that when the defense of entrapment is at issue, the government must prove beyond a reasonable doubt that the defendant was disposed to commit the criminal act "prior to first being approached by Government agents." Consequently, the majority stated, although *D* "had become predisposed to break the law by May, 1987 [the date of purchase], . . . the Government did not prove that this predisposition was independent and not the product of the attention that the Government had directed at [*D*] since . . . 1985."

The Court considered the lawful purchase of the *Bare Boys* magazines as "scant if any proof of [*D*]'s predisposition to commit an illegal act. . . ." Their purchase "may indicate a predisposition to view sexually–oriented photographs that are responsive to [*D*'s] sexual tastes; but evidence that merely indicates a generic inclination to act within a broad range, not all of which is criminal, is of little probative value in establishing predisposition." As Justice White explained, "[e]vidence of predisposition to do what once was lawful is not, by itself, sufficient to show predisposition to do what is now illegal, for there is a common understanding that most people obey the law even when they disapprove of it."

If *D* was not "ready and willing" to purchase child pornography when the government first contacted him, why did he do so when they sent him the catalogues? The majority explained:

> [T]he strong arguable inference is that, by waving the banner of individual rights and disparaging the legitimacy and constitutionality of efforts to restrict the availability of sexually explicit materials, the Government not only excited [*D*'s] interest in sexually explicit materials banned by law but also exerted substantial pressure on petitioner to obtain and read such material as part of a fight against censorship. . . .[10.2]

Does *Jacobson* have long–term significance? Perhaps. The dissent fears that the Court's ruling

> has the potential to be misread . . . as requiring that the Government must have sufficient evidence of a defendant's predisposition before it ever seeks to contact him. Surely the Court cannot intend to impose such a requirement, for it would mean that the Government must have a reasonable suspicion of criminal activity before it begins an investigation. . . .

However, there is language in the majority opinion to support such a reading, or one similar to it. For example, Justice White stated that "[t]his long–established standard [that the accused must be predisposed prior to contact with law enforcement officers] in no way encroaches upon Government investigatory techniques," thereafter quoting from the Attorney General's Guidelines on F.B.I. Undercover Operations, which provide that inducements should not be offered unless "there is a reasonable indication . . . that the subject is engaging, has engaged, or is likely to engage in illegal activity of a similar type," and which states that sting operations should be structured "so that there is reason for believing that persons drawn to the opportunity . . . are predisposed to engage in the contemplated illegal activity."

[10.2] But, as the dissent pointed out, *D* "was offered only two opportunities to buy child pornography [from the government] through the mail. Both times, he ordered." Thus, this was not a case in which the government tried to sell *D* child pornography in January, 1985, were rebuffed, and yet continued to correspond with him in an effort to induce a later sale. In this sense, *Jacobson* is factually unlike *Sherman* and *Sorrells*, in which repeated solicitations were required.

Page 359, three lines from the bottom of the page, add new footnote 15.1:

For example, in . . . an innocent person.[15.1]

[15.1] On the other hand, just as *Sherman* teaches that a person's prior predisposition to commit a crime does not necessarily prove a similar disposition at the time of the criminal activity, proof of the defendant's disposition to commit an offense at the time of the crime is not always sufficient to bar a successful entrapment claim.

In Jacobson v. United States, 112 S.Ct. 1535 (1992), discussed more fully in § 171[A] [Pock. Pt] *supra*, the Court stated that the prosecutor must prove that the defendant was disposed to commit the crime for which he was prosecuted "prior to first being approached by Government agents." Therefore, if the government contacts an innocent person, patiently "softens him up" to commit a crime, and then solicits the offense once the person is disposed to commit the offense, an entrapment claim properly lies.

§ 172 Entrapment: The Objective Test

Page 360, add at the end of footnote 19:

[19] . . . *See also* People v. Jamieson, 436 Mich 61, 461 N.W.2d 884 (1990) ("whether, under the circumstances, the governmental activity would induce a hypothetical person not ready and willing to commit the crime to engage in criminal activity.").

Page 360, add at the end of footnote 20:

[20] . . . N.D. Cent. Code 12.1–05–11(2) (entrapment occurs "when a law enforcement agent induces the commission of an offense using . . . means likely to cause normally law–abiding persons to commit the offense").

Page 361, at the end of the page, add new footnote 24.1:

They reason that . . . standards be developed.[24.1]

[24.1] *But see* State v. Sheetz, 223 N.M. 324, 825 P.2d 614 (Ct. App. 1991) (in which the court adopted a hybrid approach: prior to trial the judge determines whether the factual circumstances amount to objective entrapment and, if they do, dismisses the case; if they do not, the judge permits the jury independently to consider the entrapment defense at trial).

§ 174 Entrapment: Due Process

Page 365, end of subsection [A], add new footnote 36.1:

In the past, . . . "shocked the conscience."[36.1]

[36.1] However, in United States v. Cuervelo, 949 F.2d 559 (2nd Cir. 1991), the Court of Appeals ruled that the defendant in an international drug importation case was entitled to a hearing on her allegations of "outrageous governmental conduct," in violation of the due process clause, based on her claim that an undercover agent "sexually entrapped" her. The court stated that a hearing to dismiss the prosecution would be appropriate if she showed that the "government consciously set out to use sex as a weapon in its investigatory arsenal, or acquiesced in such conduct for its purposes upon learning that such a relationship existed," that the agent initiated the sexual relationship or allowed it to continue in order to further the investigation, and that the relationship was "entwined" with the criminal events.

Page 365, delete all of the words following the colon on line 2 of subsection [B], through the end of line 3, and substitute the following:

. . . an undercover agent arranged for *D* to sell heroin to another government agent.

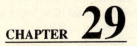

CHAPTER 29

THE RIGHT TO COUNSEL: AT TRIAL AND ON APPEAL

§ 178 The Right of Self–Representation

Page 379, add at the end of footnote 45:

[45] . . . *See* State v. Green, 238 Neb. 328, 470 N.W.2d 736 (1991) (holding that "no formal-istic litany" is needed to show that an accused knowingly and intelligently waived her right to counsel, but that she must be warned of the dangers and disadvantages of self–representation).

§ 179 The Right to Representation by One's Preferred Attorney

Page 381, add to footnote 51:

[51] . . . Feeney and Jackson, *Public Defenders, Assigned Counsel, Retained Counsel: Does the Type of Criminal Defense Counsel Matter?*, 22 Rutgers L.J. 361 (1991).

§ 181 Effective Assistance of Counsel: General Principles

Page 384, add at the end of footnote 78:

[78] . . . Furthermore, a too–frequent problem in capital cases is that court–appointed private attorneys are compensated so poorly for their services that they are disinclined to represent their clients with vigor. *See Snoozing, Unprepared Lawyer Cited*, 77 A.B.A. Journal (Feb. 1991) at 14. In order to increase the quality of appellate legal representation, the United States Supreme Court recently increased to $5,000 from $2,500 the cap on compensation of lawyers appointed to represent indigent capital appellants in that court. In re Berger, 111 S.Ct. 628 (1991).

The economic realities of representing indigent defendants in non–capital cases is even worse. A national survey completed in 1990 indicates that, for lawyers conscripted to represent non–capital indigents, the authorized rates for representation generally do not exceed $35–per–hour. Worse, many states have an overall compensation cap, *e.g.*, $500 (North Carolina, Oklahoma, South Carolina, and Tennessee). Schulhofer, *Access to Justice for the American Underclass*, The World & I, June, 1991, at 463, 471–72 (reporting data from a study completed by the Spangenberg Group).

Page 387, line 3, add new footnote 83.1:

On the other hand, . . . is less difficult.[83.1]

[83.1] Ignorance of the law, of course, is not the only non–strategy form of incompetency that may be alleged. Constitutional deficiency is shown if the defendant proves that her lawyer frequently slept during trial or during significant pre–trial hearings. *E.g.*, Ross v. Kemp, 260 Ga. 312, 393 S.E. 2d 244 (1990) and Harrison v. Zant, No. 88–V–1460 (reported in *Snoozing, Unprepared Lawyer Cited*, 77 A.B.A. Journal (Feb. 1991) at 14) (in which death sentences were overturned due to the inadequacy of an 83–year–old counsel's representation, upon proof that he slept a "good deal" during the proceedings).

§ 182 Effective Assistance of Counsel: Conflicts of Interest

Page 389, add at the end of footnote 90:

[90] . . . *See also* Shongutsie v. State, 827 P.2d 361 (Wyo. 1992) (under the state constitution, prejudice is presumed in all instances of multiple representation of criminal defendants, including those in which no objection is made by the defendant or her attorney; in the absence of appropriate waiver, multiple representation constitutes reversible error).

CHAPTER **30**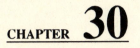

PRETRIAL RELEASE OF THE DEFENDANT

§ 185   Pretrial Release: Interests at Stake

Page 394, line 6, add new footnote 8.1:

The community also . . . they are free.[8.1]

[8.1] For example, in a study of felony case filings in February, 1988 in the 75 largest counties in the nation, 18% of the released defendants were known to have been re–arrested for a felony while free. Of this group, about two–thirds were released again after their re–arrest. U.S. Department of Justice, Pretrial Release of Felony Defendants, 1988 (Bureau of Justice Statistics, Feb. 1991).

§ 188   Preventive Detention

Page 398, add to footnote 31:

[31] . . . Miller & Guggenheim, *Pretrial Detention and Punishment*, 75 Minn. L. Rev. 335 (1990).

Page 398, add at the end of footnote 33:

[33] . . . This is not so at the state level. In a study of state felony case filings in February, 1988, in the 75 largest counties in the nation, about one–third of the defendants were not released prior to trial. Of that group, only 10% were preventively detained under state law; the remainder were unable to post required bond. U.S. Department of Justice, Pretrial Release of Felony Defendants, 1988 (Bureau of Justice Statistics, Feb. 1991).

CHAPTER **31**

PLEA BARGAINING AND GUILTY PLEAS

§ 191 Plea Bargaining: General Principles

Page 407, add to footnote 9:

[9] . . . Schulhofer & Nagel, *Negotiated Pleas Under the Federal Sentencing Guidelines: The First Fifteen Months*, 27 Am. Crim. L. Rev. 231 (1989).

§ 192 Plea Bargaining: Policy Debate

Page 408, add to footnote 20:

[20] . . . Easterbrook, *Plea Bargaining as Compromise*, 101 Yale L.J. 1969 (1992); Schulhofer, *Plea Bargaining as Disaster*, 101 Yale L.J. 1979 (1992); Scott & Stuntz, *Plea Bargaining as Contract*, 101 Yale L.J. 1909 (1992).

§ 195 Validity of a Guilty Plea: Constitutional Principles

Page 418, line 5, add new footnote 66.1:

Furthermore, ". . . of actual guilt."[66.1]

[66.1] However, the *Alford* Court warned that its "holding does not mean that a trial judge must accept every constitutionally valid guilty plea merely because a defendant wishes to plead." The Court did not explore the scope of the trial judge's discretion to reject factually–based guilty pleas, but some lower courts have done so. *See, e.g.*, United States v. Cox, 923 F.2d 519 (7th Cir. 1991) (and the cases cited therein) (in which the court upheld the trial judge's refusal to accept a factually–based guilty plea, where the defendant's statements "raised the specter that he was pleading to one crime in order to assuage his guilt for a different, uncharged crime").

§ 196 Obtaining a Guilty Plea: Federal Procedures

Page 419, line 3, add new footnote 69.1 after the word "plea":

Rule 11(f) . . . basis for the plea."[69.1]

[69.1] Although a judge must not accept a guilty plea in the absence of a factual basis, she has discretion to reject a factually–based guilty plea. *See* n. 66.1 *supra*.

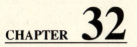
DOUBLE JEOPARDY

§ 201 Reprosecution After An Acquittal

Page 439, add to footnote 62:

[62] . . . Office of Legal Policy, U.S. Dep't of Justice, Truth in Criminal Justice Series, Report No. 6, Report to the Attorney General on Double Jeopardy and Government Appeals of Acquittals, *reprinted in* 22 U. Mich. J.L. Ref. 831 (1989).

§ 205 Multiple Prosecutions of the "Same Offense"

Page 447, add to footnote 112:

[112] . . . Locke, *On Leo Katz, Double Jeopardy, and the Blockburger Test*, 9 Law & Philosophy 295 (1991); Thomas, *A Modest Proposal to Save the Double Jeopardy Clause*, 69 Wash. U.L.Q. 195 (1991).

Page 449, add at the end of footnote 120:

[120] . . . *See generally* Poulin, *Double Jeopardy: Grady and Dowling Stir the Muddy Waters*, 43 Rutgers L. Rev. 889 (1991).

Page 451, immediately preceding subsection [D], add the following new subsection [C][3]:

[3] Post–*Grady* Jurisprudence

Lower federal courts and state courts have struggled since 1990 to determine the thrust of *Grady v. Corbin*. In *United States v. Felix*,[122.1] the Supreme Court examined *Grady* for the first time and, in the process, narrowed its scope somewhat.

In *Felix*, D operated a facility in Oklahoma at which he illegally manufactured methamphetamine. In July, 1987, federal agents raided the building and closed it, but D avoided immediate capture. Shortly thereafter, D ordered additional chemicals for use in his drug activities and had them delivered to him at a hotel at which he was staying in Missouri. D was arrested shortly thereafter.

D was prosecuted twice, first in Missouri, and later in Oklahoma. In Missouri, he was indicted for attempting to manufacture methamphetamine, based upon the delivery of the chemicals to him in that state. In order to prove D's criminal intent,

---

[122.1] 112 S.Ct 1377 (1992).

which *D* denied, the government introduced evidence of *D*'s drug manufacturing activities in Oklahoma at the raided facility. *D* was convicted.

Subsequently, *D* was prosecuted in Oklahoma on eight counts of an indictment charging him, along with others, with one count of conspiracy to manufacture, possess, and distribute methamphetamine, and with seven related substantive drug offenses. At *D*'s trial, the government introduced some of the evidence that was used against him in the Missouri trial. *D* was convicted of all eight counts.

The Tenth Circuit reversed *D*'s conviction on five of the substantive drug charges and on the conspiracy charge. It did so on the basis of the key language in *Grady*, quoted at the end of page 449 of the Main Volume, namely, that the double jeopardy clause bars a second prosecution where "to establish an essential element of an offense charged in that prosecution, the government will prove conduct that constitutes an offense for which the defendant has already been prosecuted."

The Supreme Court unanimously reversed the judgment of the Tenth Circuit. Regarding the substantive charges, the Court accused the lower court of "an extravagant reading of *Grady*."

Notice how *Felix* differs from *Grady*. In *Grady*, *D* pleaded guilty to two traffic offenses culminating from a single course of conduct, after which the government sought to prosecute *D* again, this time for a death that arose from the same traffic–offense conduct. The second prosecution was barred because the government intended to establish an element of the homicide offense – *mens rea* – by proving the conduct that constituted the two driving offenses already prosecuted.

In *Felix*, however, as the Supreme Court observed, "[t]he actual crimes charged in each case were different in both time and place; there was absolutely no common conduct linking the alleged offenses." In the first trial, *D* was charged with attempted drug manufacture in Missouri; in the second trial, he was prosecuted for substantive offenses committed at the raided facility in Oklahoma. Nowhere in *Grady* does the Court suggest that the double jeopardy clause is violated merely because of a partial overlap in evidentiary proof in separate prosecutions of different offenses. Indeed, *Grady* expressly disclaimed that it was adopting a "same evidence" or "actual evidence" test of the double jeopardy clause.[122.2]

D's misconduct in Oklahoma, later prosecuted in that state, was admissible at the Missouri trial under Federal Evidence Code 404(b), in order to prove *D*'s criminal intent as to the Missouri offense. If it had been upheld, the Tenth Circuit's ruling would have eviscerated this rule of evidence. *Felix* expressly stated that the Court did not intend such a far–reaching result: "[T]he introduction of relevant evidence of particular misconduct in a case is not the same thing as prosecution for that conduct."[122.3]

[122.2] *Grady*, 110 S.Ct. at 2093 n.12.

[122.3] The Court implicitly so held in *Dowling v. United States*, 493 U.S. 342 (1990), which was decided a few months before *Grady*. In *Dowling*, the Court upheld against a claim of collateral estoppel the introduction of prior–misconduct evidence in a criminal trial, although the defendant had previously been acquitted of the prior misconduct. *See* § 207[B] *infra*. As pointed out in *Felix*, "it is clear that [the Supreme Court] would not have had to reach the collateral–estoppel question if the mere introduction, pursuant to Rule 404(b), . . . constituted a second prosecution of that crime for purposes of the Double Jeopardy Clause."

The Supreme Court admitted, however, that *D*'s double jeopardy claim relating to the Oklahoma conspiracy charge "present[ed] a more difficult question than the substantive drug offenses." Of nine overt acts supporting the conspiracy charge brought in the Oklahoma trial, two were based on conduct for which *D* had been prosecuted in Missouri. In a portion of the opinion for which there were seven votes, Chief Justice Rehnquist stated that a literal reading of the key *Grady* language, "taken out of context," supported the Tenth Circuit's judgment.

The Supreme Court could have reached the result that it did, *i.e.*, that the double jeopardy clause was not violated, consistent with the language of *Grady*. It might have drawn a distinction, for example, between "establishing" an essential element of an offense and merely "supporting" it. Also, as Justices Stevens and Blackmun pointed out in their concurrence, there is no overt–act requirement in the federal drug conspiracy statute. Consequently, the Court could have argued that the overt–act evidence from Missouri was not introduced to "establish an *essential element*" of the conspiracy charge in Oklahoma. On the other hand, *D* might have responded that the overt–act evidence was introduced in order to prove the conspiratorial agreement in Oklahoma, the gist of the conspiracy charge.

Instead of engaging in such subtleties, the Court candidly took a different route. It observed that:

> [L]ong antedating any of these [*Blockburger*–type] cases, and not questioned in any of them, is the rule that a substantive crime, and a conspiracy to commit that crime, are not the "same offense" for double jeopardy purposes. . . .

> Faced with the necessity of reconciling this longstanding authority with our language in *Grady*, we choose to adhere to the . . . line of cases dealing with the distinction between conspiracy to commit an offense and the offense itself. These are separate offenses for double jeopardy purposes.

Consequently, the Court held that "in this case, the conspiracy charge against [*D*] was an offense distinct from any crime for which he had been previously prosecuted, and the Double Jeopardy Clause did not bar his prosecution on that charge."

Page 451, add at the beginning of footnote 124:

[124] *See* People v. Bush, 187 Mich.App. 316, 466 N.W.2d 736 (1991) (*D* was convicted of attempted murder of *V*, during the commission of a felony; four years later, *V* died when he was the victim of another assault, this time by *X*; based on evidence that *V*'s death was the result of injury to his heart caused in the original attempted murder, *D* was prosecuted for felony–murder of *V*; the court held that the *Brown* exception applied to these facts). . . .

TABLE OF CASES

[References are to sections of this Pocket Part]

[References are to sections of this Pocket Part]

INDEX

A

C

D

(Matthew Bender & Co., Inc.)

H

I

J

M

P

[References are to sections of this Pocket Part]

PLEA BARGAINING (See GUILTY PLEAS)

PRETRIAL RELEASE
Interests at stake 185
Preventive detention 188

PROBABLE CAUSE
Gates test of 46
Sliding-scale debate regarding 48

R

REASONABLE SUSPICION
Flight, as type of 95
Types of information allowed
     Personal observations 95
When not required 102

RETROACTIVITY
Current constitutional law of 11
"New rule" defined 11

ROADBLOCKS
Sobriety checkpoints 102

S

"SEARCH"
Banking records 34
Contraband, testing for 36
Conversations 32
Dog sniffs 36

SEARCH INCIDENT TO LAWFUL ARREST
Belton analyzed 72
Warrant exception, in general 68

SEARCH WARRANTS
"Neutral and detached magistrate" 51
Perjury, problem of 51, 120
Warrant clause, constitutional role of 49

"SEIZURE"
Definition of
     Persons "seized" 40
     Pursuit, as means of 40

[References are to sections of this Pocket Part]

(Matthew Bender & Co., Inc.)